POETRY

"God doesn't give me dreams to drive me crazy."

-Jalaysha Malik

2017

I would like to thank my entire family. Especially my mom Julia, my dad Derrick and my sisters Emilia, Madison, and Parker. I Love You, Thank You.

This book is dedicated to all generations who have lost their life due to enormous amounts of social injustice. Gone but never forgotten.

SALTED CARAMEL

PROLOGUE

When life is met with trouble, some would say we will feel, gritty, mad, angry or even salty.

When life is met with accomplishment some would say life is wondrous, happy, content or even sweet.

And when we are experiencing both we are being fulfilled with anger and happiness.

We are facing difficulty in the eye at home, work, or school.

While, then facing pleasure in the eye at home, work, or school.

Possibly even pleasure and difficulty at the same time, in the same place, of the same hour.

We are attaining the most popular polar emotions that life can give us.

And with this, what are we supposed to do? How are we supposed to react? or How are we supposed to cope with this gyrate of emotions?

We live in the present and not a moment further, making the best out of now with the worst situation.

Making sugar through salt today and blessing tomorrow.

Because the life that lives within us and the life we see around us is nothing less than Salted Caramel.

POEMS

06

PAST

Kings and Queens

My struggle is glorified in the eyes of your people

My strength is forsaken and hidden in the shadows

My hard-work is belittled and minimized to comfort the eye of man

Apparently, I was born out of slavery and my ancestors before

Lies,

I was not bred from beatings and the authority of white man

I stand on any land as a queen

I come from jewels, peace, leadership, and beauty

Strategist, war heroes, inventors, cunning confidence

My divine grace could not be built on a boat or in the fields of cotton

Our elements are too amiable to only be recognized for subjugation

My history is Kings and Queens

They tore off our wreaths

Only so, we can wear our crowns higher than before

My hair, an emblem of endearment and royalty

Our history of Kings and Queens

We Are Inevitable.

Tribe

"A dread from the bottom of the boat, you worthless animal."

"Beautiful young African Queen, ravishing, strong, glowing damsel."

How could I know which is true?

How could I believe either side?

What am I?

They stole me from my home land,

They captured me and put me on the edge of death

They ripped me from the region I convene "Accueil"

My village

My tribe

Now I'm scum and suffering, death will come soon

Alone and bare, no one by my side

I hold onto my dignity and my pride

One day I will go back when I'm granted freedom

But, Lord knows freedom is only existent in the blue moon, so maybe I'll visit in my dreams

I don't call him "master"

He's a thief of my culture

But they sold me...

For rum and for guns

So I am an animal, nothing more than a product

I've realized my worth

I wish someone were near to tell me I've been mistaken

But I know I'm not

Why be alive, why be breathing

Only to witness the treacherous conditions and horrible fate
that has cast upon my brothers and sisters

Today will be my last day surviving

Today will be the day I set my self-free

And go to my homeland

My tribe,

For the rest of eternity.

Good Life

Suffocation

Suicide

Uprisings

But, we have a good life

That's what they said, that is what they told us

Christianity

They saved us

From war...

But the passage was a war, a worse war

Not against opposing defendants, but a fight for my life

But, we have a good life

I cannot complain

I reside by my mother's side, as much others do not

She holds me tight and whispers every night

"I will never lose you."

But on the ship with no room to turn, she fainted, passed out

So, I whispered

"I almost lost you."

But, we have a good life

Master only whipped us four times a day

For no exact reason, but others had it much worse

Master seemed to like me especially

Touching me in ways I feel I should shriek, screech, yell but I
do not

Because he gave me this life

Mommy screams when she hears

He hits her harder and I start to cry

So, I yell...

"WE HAVE A GOOD LIFE"

He backs away, I've learned my lesson

"You're mine, I own you! My property."

But, we have a good life

Wait

What is freedom?

Civil

Beatings and lashes we took them all,

Water hoses and police dogs, just to tell that we stood tall

Marches for days, just so we can integrate

And speeches for years,

So our broken down spirits won't turn into tears.

We put up a fight to let them know, that they can push us away but we will never go

Back of the bus and back of the line

Walking down the street with chills rolling down my spine,

Sitting in jails just to prove a point

Hoping that rallies without violence were the first checkpoint

But they hated our skin and so we suffered

Only making our inside and minds much tougher.

They never knew

This part of history they left behind,

Saying after the 13th amendment I was free and my life was mine

Only if you knew how slavery still lived in the depths of time

And how they leased us for crimes that weren't even crimes

Then they sold us to the mines

We had to work for free

With no food or health amenities

They said after the 13th I would be free

But they flipped the script and left me as a convict for my life to be leased

And here I wonder what I ever did to serve such fate

For I went to working in fields to hard labor date by date

What really makes me bawl is that I did nothing wrong

When I was working in the fields I thought about freedom and I sung the song

Then my time came

And they found another way to have me as a slave by another name

The textbooks don't show that even after the 13th I wasn't free to go.

Maybe

I remember when they put me in jail for walking on the street

I was in the way so the swept me off my feet

But not the way you guessed it

They smashed my face on the ground and yelled at me fiercely "YOU ARE ARRESTED!"

And everything I say can and will be used against me

But I spoke that I did nothing wrong and to please let me be

Please let me free

Yet I ended up at the precinct and they were questioning my plea

I was just so confused and amused by the way they took me away

Left me thinking I will never be okay

Now don't get me wrong I been roughed up before

But not the way I was belittled and crying on the floor

Only because I was walking on the street

Maybe...

If I went another way they wouldn't have swept me off my feet

Remember

I almost forgot to tell you twice that you come from a queen,

That your royalty and grace is everything

And your king covered in chocolate is great too

I love the way you dance and represent your hairdo

You even smell like royalty

Your heart is filled with loyalty

Only if they knew that my history is filled with you

Whatever era you claim just remember that you came from a queen,

A queen who lived long before and helped to raise the earth when it was poor

Her heart is poured into you

Boy or girl, the queen is within you

Away from the history that was forgotten, when they filled our heads with cotton

We didn't look past and see

Our past is filled with royalty

16

PRESENT

A Wish

Unarmed but you take him down

Unarmed but he's on the ground

Unarmed but we're mourning at his crown

Unarmed but his life is gone

Unarmed but your shot was dead-on

The news crew knows

But they refuse to show

That he was unarmed yet they still took the blow

And I was torn

By the rivers born, on the side of my face

Because of their unfaithful grace

And everyone sees

That his life was taken with ease

Crouching at his knees

Just wishing they were unarmed.

AWAY

Dear Pops,

I know you're all alone

and mama told me about the police, she said they wrecked our home

Cause they stole you from us and they took your throne

Mama says you were a hardworking man, could never hurt a fly

Somehow, you're still guilty somehow, it's all a lie

But I sat confused staring at the bars,

The police are supposed to protect me, yet that seemed so far

Mama said they'd do anything to put a black man in jail

No matter the consequence, no matter the bail

It wasn't about home, family, or life

It was about something far more disgusting; race subjugation, price

I will never understand why my pops is gone

I will never understand why they use our lives as a pawn.

<u>Markings</u>

In society, we are presented standards

No, we don't have to follow, uniqueness is key!

But, be too unique and you'll fall beneath

There is a weight range that we see

No, you don't have to be that size, thick is in!

But, be too thick and you'll lose everything within

Styles are shown! Nu uh you don't have to wear that,

Thrifty is cool!

But, be too thrifty and you'll be looked at as a fool

We live in standards

Standards set by people who are seemingly better,

Until you realize we are all raised in the same skeleton

We allow people to bash us because we are diverse

Even though diversity is the beauty of the universe

It's sad, you see...

Everyone would rather be someone else

When someone else would rather be them

Thinking we live in an alternate universe where,

the only thing missing is the beauty within.

Always remember to let your melanin pop

Remember to be you, that is something that can never be
stopped

Lost

#findourgirls (A tribute to all the girls that are missing in DC and all around the world).

There are tears on the streets of the capital,

And no it's not rain.

Our beautiful melanin girls are crying out in vain,

Every night and day, how can we allow them to endure such pain?

Our souls cry out and yelp,

As they stand on the sideline with no desire to help.

I don't know how much more pain we have to face,

Will they ever embrace that our rights have been lost and our paramour's forgotten as they liberate our grace?

How can it be that #AllLivesMatter

But that accusation is only true,

When we are fighting for rights that come to benefit you.

WHY?!

You took my heart, you took my soul, you took my goals

Without even asking why you took my life

Without even wondering who, you took my family too

Without even questioning first you took my purpose and my worth

And with me crying so loud, you took my beautiful sound

I am not complaining that I reside with God

I'm just wondering why you took my future and goals everyone would be proud of

I really had dreams you know...

I was going to go far and soar high, really high though

But I never had the chance to grow up, so

You took my heart, you took my soul, you took my goals

Ripped me of my pride and took me from my mother's side

Why am I less than any other kid?

Why did you take my life the way you did?

A message to you, just to let you know, that I would've been brighter than you would have ever thought

But too soon, it was my time to go.

Be Proud

The whole community should be respected and reflected
because we're all one

No matter what we dress like or come from

We should all represent one another

There is no fight if we can't stand together as brothers

Because every time I go into a store they look at me funny

Making sure I have money

But why is that though?

Who made the stereotype saying I was a thief on the low?

Anyways, look there's so much more to us

We can be doctors, artist, scientist and a whole bunch of stuff

I know the stereotypes get you down

But you're not a thug and you don't need to sag around town

Getting your education is cool

Walk out with a degree and make them look like fools

But really, let's think

Why do we let these stereotypes get us down?

After all, we been through we can't be pushed around

Tell your momma you will make her proud

Be the royalty that you are, and don't shift your crown.

It Hurts

I will never forget what I see on the news

It gives me chills and makes me blue

Because that represents so much more than "Little boy was shot on the floor"

The headlines don't suffice the brutality in life

What is even worse is that some people don't see that children deserve to experience everything

No matter their color or sex they like

They deserve everything nice and beautiful to sight

So that's why the news frightens me

Every time I turn it on it's like a new episode of "shot by he"

And I know I'm not the only one that cries whenever someone mentions a gun

I only start to think of the people that lost everything over something dumb

It all really makes no sense to me

How can we wake up in the morning and expect peace?

Honestly, I do not know

But I know the violence must go.

24

FUTURE

<u>Together</u>

We can't sit back and act like it never happened

We keep moving forward until we're marching and rapping

About how we overcame the supremacy of the whites

And how we led our fight through the night

How we never gave up despite,

the tragedies that led us crying on sight

How we are united as one

How we decided to stand tall and reach for the sun

How we never fell behind the white lines of race

And how we took this and led it at our own pace

How dare they think the past is what we'll hold onto

We have to shift to the future and make it brand new

Open your eyes to realize that fate has us fighting every day to take back what we struggled with date to date

No man deserves to be confined and hidden behind bars and mines

So, what are we going to do?

There are no more excuses to spill

The fate of the eternity depends on you.

Don't be Afraid

What more can I say?

I can't tell you how to live your life I can't tell you what to do today

But what I do know is your life could be better

We could be singing together and brightening the weather

Because we believe

That the future is us and yes, it'll be tough but we'll take our fighting chance and we won't bluff

We lift one another up and scream because if we are side by side we're a team

You might be thinking it can't be me but when that light beams on the rear end of your tire even though you didn't do anything.

You'll be wishing you fought for more and clawed your way through the doors of what we don't have

So the future generations can see what we did and not be suppressed, thinking how nothing ever changed, laying and feeling bad

We can build this empire again because we're strong enough to do it hand by hand, no stopping till' we win

And I'm not saying read these lines and be inspired for a short amount of time but really sit and think, we can do anything

And anything we can do.

But it all starts with you

So, don't be afraid, we're creating the future now

Get up and spread the word throughout your whole town

This world is ours and we will overcome

Everything they ever destroyed in the long run

Fight True

Now I know we can do it, fight true

But the way we fight still depends on you

Violence is not the way for we must kill them with kindness

Or they will shelter us with blindness

It's not right to fight fire with fire so we must bring back the thoughts
of the king and rise higher

They expect the worse for our rallies and marches so we must stand
tall and double our arches

We must let them know the only thing we'll be shooting is truth

Something that no one can bulletproof

It's essential for us to see that our background and stereotypes are
not everything

The ways were embedded but now we are headed for a higher road

We can let the pain and the weakness go

We are free to let all know

Our truth is what kills,

So, don't second guess it

We're in the future but the records we will bring up will be reckless

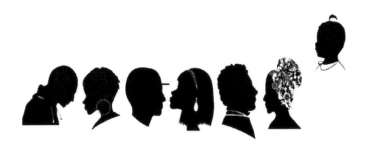

When?

Now or never?

The question stands true because who is better to fight for your rights than you?

We're going to make it so that you don't have to be shot down for your name to get around

But for you to stand tall and everyone will know that you put up the biggest brawl

You spoke truth like no one knew you had it in you

Now they can't do anything but sit back and listen to how your story is within you

No guns, tasers, or weapons, we leave them all

We let our stories ring the minds of the racist until they fall

Come on now you can do it

Tell your feelings until you the fire rises in you, now you're doing it

No pressure, wait, you're doing fine

But always think to yourself "I'm me and my life is mine".

<u>You, only you</u>

Your power is displayed with a pump of a fist,

Your mind is filled with strength and your beauty with bliss

You're admirable from all perspectives

Best thing you can be is you

So, fight for what you believe in and,

See it through.

Last thing

Now I have one last poem to leave with you

And you may be thinking this chapter is the shortest of them all

But I'm leaving you two blank pages to write how you will stand tall

And this may seem silly I know,

But don't forget that no matter what you can always be the first to grow

The first to fight for what you believe in and reap the benefits until the very end

The history is what brought us here today

So, I must say our ancestors paved the way

But why stop at what seems fine

We can push and be great beyond all lines

You have the flame in you

It shines bright and burns in sight

Never forget what you witnessed

You lead a journey of life

And now you can add some pages in to a positive light

Don't think too heavily on the things that you're afraid of

But the things you want to fight and get rid of

Everyone deserves to fight with kindness and see good always wins

Everyone also deserves to fight their own way until they see their bright end

So, let these two pages know

Everything in your mind

Be free and it's okay to let go.